PRIVATE LESSONS

Jazz
HANON

By Peter Deneff

for
George V. Deneff

ISBN 0-634-06666-8

7777 W. BLUEMOUND RD. P.O. BOX 13819 MILWAUKEE, WI 53213

In Australia Contact:
Hal Leonard Australia Pty. Ltd.
22 Taunton Drive P.O. Box 5130
Cheltenham East, 3192 Victoria, Australia
Email: ausadmin@halleonard.com

Visit Hal Leonard Online at
www.halleonard.com

About the author

Peter Deneff is a pianist, composer, and teacher in Southern California. He began playing at age three and started his formal training at nine with classical pianist Leaine Gibson. He began jazz studies in 1986 with pianist Mike Garson. He studied composition at California State University Long Beach with Dr. Justus Matthews and Dr. Martin Herman. He is currently earning his masters degree in music composition at CSULB, doing studio work, recording discs for the Yamaha Disklavier piano, composing, studying and writing film scores, and performing with his band Excursion as well as with other groups. He also teaches privately and at Cypress College. He resides in Southern California with his wife Diane, and his children Gitana, George, and Sophia.

Introduction

When a piano student embarks on the study of jazz piano, they are beginning a multifaceted journey into the worlds of harmony, rhythm, melody, and improvisation. There is more than one "correct way" to study any of these skills and a multitude of texts that explore the various topics. This text deals with the systematic programming of the fingers to automate the playing of jazz chord voicings. In the same way that *Jazz Hanon* automates and strengthens the fingers through the playing of melodic lines, the following exercises will increase proficiency in the playing of chords. By practicing chords in this manner, the pianist will gain the ability to navigate complex harmonic progressions with increased facility and ease.

Besides being a physical exercise, this text will also serve as a mental exercise in more than one way. Primarily, the student will learn to recognize chord tones, progressions, and intervals in all keys. In addition, it is highly recommended that the student label all the chords throughout the book using proper jazz chord symbols. In this way, they will not only reinforce their sight recognition of chords, but also be able to practice the voicings while reading the symbols, thus preparing for reading lead sheets.

The text is to be practiced sequentially. By mastering the exercises from beginning to end, the pianist will follow a logical course of study that builds upon previously learned material. Students should observe the following guidelines when practicing these studies.

- Back should be straight with shoulders relaxed.
- Hands should be low profile with fingers curved.
- Always practice with a metronome, sequencer or drum machine.
- Tempo should be as fast as the exercise can be performed *accurately*.
- Playing should be accurate and even.
- Don't forget to breathe and relax.

While these exercises are certainly challenging, students will enjoy the sound and feel of the voicings. Musicians must be able to enjoy the process of developing proficiency as well as the results. By practicing this text diligently and purposefully, pianists will attain their goals and master the skill of voicing jazz chords.

Happy practicing!
Peter Deneff

3-Voice ii-V-I Progressions

1

2

3

4

5

6

3-Voice Diatonic Progression

7

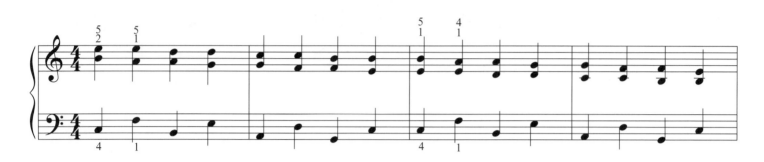

9

3-Voice Harmonized Major Scales

8

3-Voice Dominant Seventh Cycle
9

3-Voice Descending ii-V Progressions
10

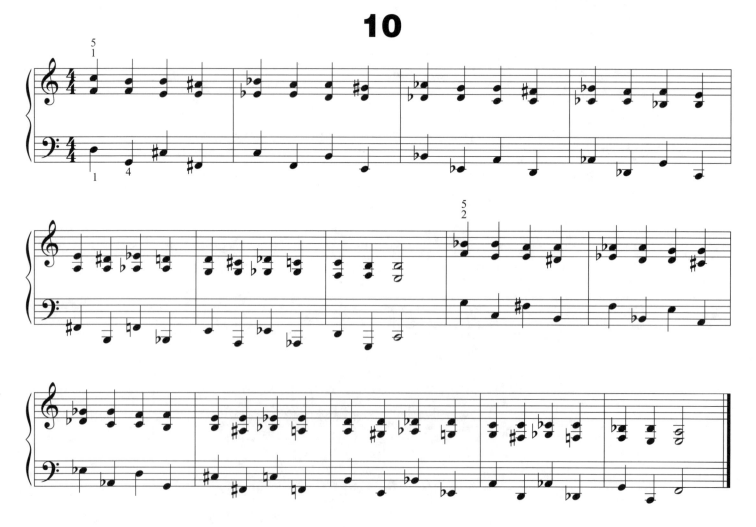

3-Voice Minor ii°-V-i Progression

11

12

13

14

15

16

3-Voice Minor Diatonic Progression
17

19

3-Voice Harmonized Minor Scales
18

3-Voice Descending Major Sevenths
19

3-Voice Descending Minor Sevenths
20

4-Voice ii-V-I Progressions
21

22

23

24

25

26

4-Voice Diatonic Progression
27

4-Voice Harmonized Major Scales
28

4-Voice Dominant Seventh Cycle
29

4-Voice Descending ii-V Progression
30

4-Voice Minor ii°-V-i Progressions

31

32

33

34

35

36

4-Voice Minor Diatonic Progression
37

4-Voice Harmonized Minor Scales
38

4-Voice Descending Major Sevenths
39

4-Voice Descending Minor Sevenths
40

5-Voice ii-V-I Progressions
41

42

43

44

45

46

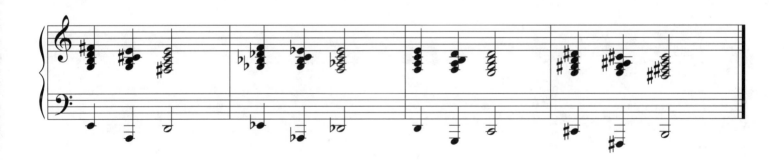

5-Voice Diatonic Progression
47

5-Voice Harmonized Major Scales
48

5-Voice Dominant Seventh Cycle
49

5-Voice Descending ii-V Progression

50

5-Voice Minor ii°-V-i Progressions

51

52

53

54

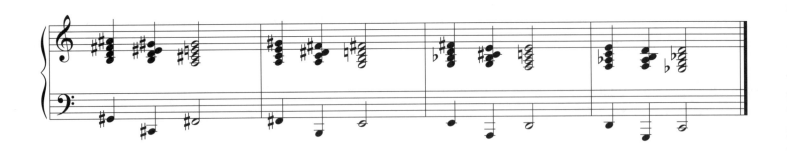

55

5-Voice Minor Diatonic Progression
57

5-Voice Harmonized Minor Scales
58

5-Voice Descending Major Sevenths
59

5-Voice Descending Minor Sevenths
60

5-Voice Dominant Seventh Cycle (with ♭9)

61

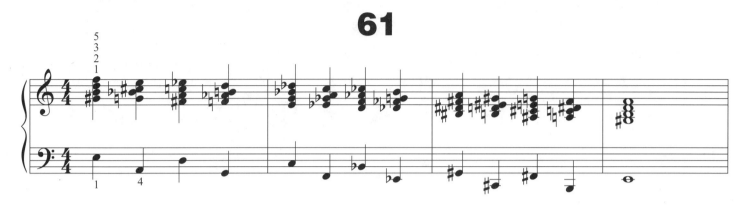

5-Voice Altered Dominant Seventh Cycle

62

4-Voice Altered Dominant Seventh Cycle
63

5-Voice Altered Dominant Seventh Cycle
64

4-Voice Altered Dominant Seventh Cycle
65

5-Voice ii-V-I Progressions
(with Alterations)
66

69

70

Musicians Institute Press

is the official series of Southern California's renowned music school, Musicians Institute. **MI** instructors, some of the finest musicians in the world, share their vast knowledge and experience with you – no matter what your current level. For guitar, bass, drums, vocals, and keyboards, **MI Press** offers the finest music curriculum for higher learning through a variety of series:

ESSENTIAL CONCEPTS
Designed from MI core curriculum programs.

MASTER CLASS
Designed from MI elective courses.

PRIVATE LESSONS
Tackle a variety of topics "one-on-one" with MI faculty instructors.

KEYBOARD

Blues Hanon
by Peter Deneff • **Private Lessons**
00695708 . . . . $14.95

Dictionary of Keyboard Grooves
by Gail Johnson • **Private Lessons**
00695556 Book/CD Pack $16.95

**Funk Keyboards –
The Complete Method**
by Gail Johnson • **Master Class**
00695336 Book/CD Pack $14.95

Jazz Chord Hanon
by Peter Deneff • **Private Lessons**
00695791 . . . . $12.95

Jazz Hanon
by Peter Deneff • **Private Lessons**
00695554 . . . . $12.95

Keyboard Technique
by Steve Weingard • **Essential Concepts**
00695365 . . . . $12.95

Keyboard Voicings
by Kevin King • **Essential Concepts**
00695209 . . . . $12.95

Music Reading for Keyboard
by Larry Steelman • **Essential Concepts**
00695205 . . . . $12.95

R&B Soul Keyboards
by Henry J. Brewer • **Private Lessons**
00695327 Book/CD Pack $16.95

Rock Hanon
by Peter Deneff • **Private Lessons**
00695784 . . . . $12.95

Salsa Hanon
by Peter Deneff • **Private Lessons**
00695226 . . . . $12.95

FOR MORE INFORMATION, SEE YOUR LOCAL MUSIC DEALER,
OR WRITE TO:

HAL•LEONARD®
CORPORATION
7777 W. BLUEMOUND RD. P.O. BOX 13819 MILWAUKEE, WI 53213

Visit Hal Leonard Online at **www.halleonard.com**

DRUM

**Afro-Cuban Coordination
for Drumset**
by Maria Martinez • **Private Lessons**
00695328 Book/CD Pack $14.95

Blues Drumming
by Ed Roscetti • **Essential Concepts**
00695623 Book/CD Pack $14.95

Brazilian Coordination for Drumset
by Maria Martinez • **Master Class**
00695284 Book/CD Pack $14.95

**Chart Reading Workbook
for Drummers**
by Bobby Gabriele • **Private Lessons**
00695129 Book/CD Pack $14.95

Double Bass Drumming
by Jeff Bowders
00695723 Book/CD Pack $19.95

Drummer's Guide to Odd Meters
by Ed Roscetti • **Essential Concepts**
00695349 Book/CD Pack $14.95

**Funk & Hip-Hop Grooves
for Drums**
by Ed Roscetti • **Private Lessons**
00695679 Book/CD Pack $14.95

Latin Soloing for Drumset
by Phil Maturano • **Private Lessons**
00695287 Book/CD Pack $14.95

**Working the Inner Clock
for Drumset**
by Phil Maturano • **Private Lessons**
00695127 Book/CD Pack $16.95

WORKSHOP SERIES
Transcribed scores of the greatest songs ever!

Blues Workshop
00695137 . . . . $22.95

Classic Rock Workshop
00695136 . . . . $19.95

VOICE

Harmony Vocals
by Mike Campbell & Tracee Lewis • **Private Lessons**
00695262 Book/CD Pack $17.95

**Musician's Guide to
Recording Vocals**
by Dallan Beck • **Private Lessons**
00695626 Book/CD Pack $14.95

Sightsinging
by Mike Campbell • **Essential Concepts**
00695195 . . . . $17.95

Vocal Technique
by Dena Murray • **Essential Concepts**
00695427 Book/CD Pack $22.95

ALL INSTRUMENTS

Approach to Jazz Improvisation
by Dave Pozzi • **Private Lessons**
00695135 Book/CD Pack $17.95

Encyclopedia of Reading Rhythms
by Gary Hess • **Private Lessons**
00695145 . . . . $19.95

Going Pro
by Kenny Kerner • **Private Lessons**
00695322 . . . . $17.95

Home Recording Basics
featuring Dallan Beck
00695655 VHS Video $19.95

Harmony & Theory
by Keith Wyatt & Carl Schroeder • **Essential Concepts**
00695161 . . . . $17.95

Lead Sheet Bible
by Robin Randall and Janice Peterson •
Private Lessons
00695130 Book/CD Pack $19.95

Prices, contents, and availability subject to change without notice